D0876939

www.finishinglinepress.com

Richeldis of Walsingham

poems by

Sally Thomas

Finishing Line Press
Georgetown, Kentucky

Richeldis of Walsingham

Copyright © 2016 by Sally Thomas
ISBN 978-1-63534-025-9 First Edition
All rights reserved under International and Pan-American Copyright Conventions.
No part of this book may be reproduced in any manner whatsoever without written
permission from the publisher, except in the case of brief quotations embodied in critical
articles and reviews.

ACKNOWLEDGMENTS

Grateful acknowledgment is due the editors of the following journals, in which
the poems in this volume first appeared:

The Rialto (UK): "Offering"
Dappled Things: "Richeldis of Walsingham"

Publisher: Leah Maines

Editor: Christen Kincaid

Cover Art: Sally Thomas

Author Photo: Kelly Davenport

Cover Design: Elizabeth Maines

Printed in the USA on acid-free paper.
Order online: www.finishinglinepress.com
also available on amazon.com

Author inquiries and mail orders:
Finishing Line Press
P. O. Box 1626
Georgetown, Kentucky 40324
U. S. A.

Table of Contents

Ad Majorem Dei Gloriam

OFFERING

Temple of Sulis Minerva, at Bath

The water was not so green then.
It had a roof for a sky. And people
Drowned curses in it, and wishes.
In the glass case, a brooch of Irish
Make: a golden circle, its ends
Bitten together by two lions' heads,
Its heavy pin made to pierce
A cloak's rough weave.

Someone's hands, steady or unsteady,
Worked it backward through the fabric.
Weighed it a moment, maybe,
Considering the price of homesickness,
Memory, dowry, bartering against
A goddess who boiled deeper than her waters.
Who might be induced to remember
One name. Forgot anyway.
Lost the petition, any record of an answer.
Cherished only what the asking cost.

RICHELDIS OF WALSINGHAM

In A.D. 1061, in Norfolk, not far from the North Sea coast, Richeldis de Faverches, Lady of the Manor of Walsingham, prayed for and received three visions. In these visions the Virgin Mary appeared to her and showed her the house at Nazareth where she had received the angel Gabriel's unexpected visit.

According to legend, the Virgin gave Richeldis the exact dimensions of this holy house and a directive to build a replica of it at Walsingham. This Richeldis did, though not without some trials. As the legend has it, she tried three times, unsuccessfully, to have the house built, according to what seem to have been unclear directions concerning its location. After a night of prayer she awoke to discover that angels had built the house while she slept, on a site where a holy well was found to bubble from the ground.

Throughout the Middle Ages Walsingham, called "England's Nazareth," remained a pilgrimage site, second only to Canterbury in its volume of pious traffic. Under Henry VIII, however, the king's own barefoot pilgrimages to Walsingham notwithstanding, the shrine was destroyed in 1538, and its devotion suppressed.

A Roman Catholic shrine, in the medieval Slipper Chapel, was restored in 1934. An Anglican shrine, featuring a rebuilt Holy House on the site of the miraculous spring, had opened in the 1920s.

biddan (to pray)

There is the rope's moan on the well-lip.
There is the cold sky, cloud-combed.
There is the sea, the headland's headdress,
Folding, folding, far afield,
Sun born from barn roofs, the tree-bare rise.
There is the lick of Lauds-bell, the wind's weeping.

Biddan: Ic bidde. We bidden.
Bed-making. Bidden, the soul's housewife sweeps
Clean the clod-cold hearth, furnishes fire
To see by, with sighing more wordful than words.

So she might have written.
So she surely said—*Ic bidde. We bidden.*
So I say, because the words lie hidden.

scryn (shrine)

Through green May softness every year, the people come
Barefoot into town, calling each other *Pilgrim*
In the self-conscious way that people do
When their world's ceased believing. In a bow-
Window, forty various-sized Buddhas
Laugh at them—I wonder if they notice,
Or if the bust of Charles I above
The door opposite recalls them to what they love:
An England pocked with priest-holes, botched with blood.
Of course it was everyone's blood. It's always blood,
Blood and fire, burnt offering, the acceptable
Holocaust.
                    Here, though, there waits no *holy blisful*
Martir, only two or three bent cotton-haired
Ladies in cardigans, arm in arm. A whispered
Consultation, rooms, tea, and the public toilet,
Which might have been cleaner. Above the low houses, violet
Rainclouds bloom on the sky. In the pilgrims' hostel,
Where they've been vouchsafed a room, an American couple
Watch with mounting dismay as their two-year-old
Smears herself with red jelly and cream beneath the mild
Horrified gaze of more cardigan-armored ladies
Wearing nametags that say not *I am Church*, but *Gladys,*
Dilys, Sheila, strangers on a first-name basis,
Which perhaps after all is what the Church is—
Aliens sharing a glassy taste of holy water.
He Who Would Valiant Be. Candles that shudder
Across the Lady's gold impassive face.
A recurrent longing for something else.

richeldis
circa 1080

It's now—at this time of year—
I expect her. I sit in my low three-legged chair.

Spinning, spring firelight on the floor, pale weather.
Pear tree wreathed in dim blooms, the outer

Door propped as if at any moment someone
Might speak my name, or listen

As I sing to myself—*ic singe*—and watch this wool
Wind itself into something useful.

My hands that draw the twisted strands out long—
Blue-veined, knob-knuckled, stiffening.

My warm-flanked hounds
Sigh and twitch in the strewn rushes. All my grounds—

Little lambent curve of river, new-leafed trees
Catching at the wind as it hurries

In from the sea, hummocky meadow
Where one dun cow

Grazes her own shadow beneath the moon—
Swathed in time, my mortal earth sleeps alone.

waeter (water)

Widowhood's a long waking,
She tells herself. Past midnight
In the strange hostel bed, fingers plucking
Uneasily at the coverlet,
She watches moonlight on the wall,
Chalk-pale, feels the cold spot at her feet
Where other feet are not.

She can't recall
Any more how it felt
Even to long for the companionable heat.

Even longer since she recalled
What it might be like to long for a child.

They eat so messily.

Now there is only
Not being lonely.

Now there are parish mini-bus outings and
Fair linen to be washed, starched, ironed
To a crisp altar-shaped white wafer.

Now, alone in darkness, she prays—
Self-conscious, thinking always of what her late
Low-church mother would have said—seven Hail Marys,
Drinking the steady rhythm of her prayer
Like mother's milk, until
Sleep finds her lying wide-eyed there
And gives her black water from his well.

stangefeall (fallen stones)

Stone door on the grass, portal from here to here.
Walk around. Walk through. Wherever you go, there you are,
In an avenue of gray stone, invisibly walled.
It's quiet there, and old.
In the bluebell woods, silence
Speaks in tongues. The eloquence
Of the small river moving always forward to the unseen
Sea is like the cherubim's, clean
With the cleanliness of humility, crying
Holy, hiding their eyes.
                        These things are made for dying:
Stone, and the hand that lays it on the earth.
These things are made for birth:
Wild iris swelling among their spears,
And in the well garden, years on years,
Frogspawn glittering stickily in algae
Green and complicated as the rainy sky.

ham (home)
1918

In waning light a clattering bus sets down
One traveler beside the village pump
Where the road forks, and the curve's quiet houses
Beneath their skeletal roses sit dark-eyed.
No lamps lit yet. It's only early
Afternoon, cold and gusty. She
Has to catch her hat before an updraft sends
It winging over the old priory wall.

That anything can stand: this still surprises her.
In her dreams she's always unrolling the endless bandages
Around endless ends of arms and legs, the faces
Chewed, spat out. Blood, and blood, and blood.
She can't wash her hands enough. *Like Lady Macbeth,*
She thinks wryly—*Funny I should feel that way,*
When it's not my fault. The fault is in our stars . . .

She shakes herself and picks up her valise.
A town of women: that's what she's come home to.
Tomorrow Mother will have friends in to tea.
Nurse Cavell told me once—but no, she can't
Speak of things like that. It's over now.
Everything will be the way it was.

Mother's friends will say so over tea,
Even Mrs. Holm, whose John went walking
In the garden of the Somme—he was sown there.
Even Mrs. Carter, who lost two,
One at Verdun, one at Ypres. Her remaining
Stump, planted daily in the front window,
Speaks to no one. It's over now. Everything
Will be the way it was.

Well, there's a robin
Calling from the wall. A little flame
Of song in the cold, at home among
Gaunt archways and doors that lead to nowhere,
Stripped trees and the sharp green teeth of daffodils.
Everything will be the way it always is.
Swedes with the Sunday roast. The vicar asked.
No curate, though. There are shortages of curates.
There are shortages, as well, of faith and hope.
And love. One cannot really hope for love.

duru (door)

Does an angel need a door?
Or is he simply *there*,
Where you thought
No one was? We're taught
To count our guardian
Angels, each a person
Occupying—not space,
Exactly; he's not a physical presence—
Perhaps it's enough to say
We count them.
                                    He
More than counts. He wears
His name like a cloak of feathers:
Gabriel. Garment of fire.
Wind. A smell like fear
Or snow, that sharp blue
Outdoor scent. Who
Wouldn't startle, seeing
Him suddenly *being*
That thing we believe
In, made of knowing, and of love?

aefentid (eventide)
1882

Corset strings must be left loose, then looser.
I'm sorry, madam. I can't pull harder than that.
Never mind, Ellis. I suppose we must resign ourselves.
The light's blue above the line of roofs.
Cold settles on the china jug and basin.
Soon he'll come walking up the road
From a burial—one of these people—
Prayer book in a pocket of his coat.

My hands fly over the bowl of winter jasmine.
Ellis cut it in the garden and brought it in.
My hands are white like moths. I'll go out in the spring.
There's a smell of mutton again. Will he say, *Mutton again?*

In London now the lamplighter will be going
Down the crescent touching all the posts with flame.
They'll be laughing by the fire in the drawing room.
Here there is only quiet and the smell of mutton.
Here a gray wall molders among bare trees.
Here there is only the road that divides at the pump
And runs away over the river and down to the sea.

þrines (trinity)

Here, their little daughter kneels in a pale dress
By a clump of bluebells, a small cool fire. In this

Image you see a trinity: child looked at,
Mother, father looking. One of them has got

The camera—that the other hovers near
Can't be presumed, only hoped for.

In those wet woods, the smell of rain, river, and stone
Is an atmosphere, complete. Let's say they move in it, all three,

Father, mother, child, the little trinity
Perfect in itself, but meant to grow

More life, as the stone's-throw ripples go
Widening over the river's fluid skin

And always to the sea are hastening down.

gemynd (memory)
1659

Our house is beautiful, very square
And golden. Its tall windows stare
Straight into the sun.
In the morning I walk in the garden.
Long ago it belonged to holy men—
I think they were holy, though
They were papists, and I am not to think so.
My brother and I look sometimes for
A holy well that's supposed to be here
And isn't. There is a well garden.
The well is full of frogs' eyes, golden
As the stone of our house. The stone
Arches in the garden stand sharply alone.
I feel sorry for them.
They seem
Like people I wish I had known.

richeldis
circa 1080

To sit companionably.
To say,

And how is it with you,
While the slow

Embers tick in the fireplace, the loom
Clacks and sighs, the room

Rests like a cat curled
On the wide windowsill of the world,

Looking out
Into the strangeness of the night

From its place
Of purring peace—

Another woman to riddle
Through the dark hours with, to sit in little

Wells of silence with, when speech
Falters, and each

Reads with sure, blind fingers the text
Of her own weaving, and doesn't mind what happens next.

brecan (to break)
1538

In the night, we heard a sound of thunder.
Just now in the wet white morning light
My mother has come back from church—
Going for our water, was all she said, and
Mind you stay inside, Margery.
Keep the little ones inside, and out of the fire—

They are broken. The Mother and the Child.
Faces shattered so that they aren't faces
But only bits of stone. My mother put them
Into her yoked buckets and brought them home.
Bits and pieces. *I didn't know what to do.*
They shouldn't lie there broken in the rain.

Now they lie broken on our table.
An eye, a smile. All the saints are headless,
My mother says. Her voice is tight and dry.
When I ask where my father is today,
And what they will have done with Father Walter,
And how we all will hear the Mass without him,
She shrugs and turns again to mend the fire.
The turnips roast like heads in the coals.

fisc (fish)

Beneath the bank's overhang
Fingerlings hide:
Silver streaks, glancing
Sunlight on a road
With trees overhead,
Woven and wavering,
Touched by wind
Like a current meandering
Back, undecided,
To its spawning
Bed.

       In the church they are saying
Mass. Outside,
The world is praying.
Without a word,
The sun's tracing
Trout-shapes on mud.

halig dag (holiday)
1401

I'm run off my feet.
No: my feet are still there.
All night the blood pounds inside them.
Ale, ale. Fleas in the bed?
Well, of course there are fleas.
My own bed has fleas.
Fleas never hurt a body. Ale, ale.
You would think a drink of holy water,
Bubbling cold from the entrails of the world,
Out of mystery, tasting like metal—
If you could drink a new blade—tasting
Like the earth's true cold thin blood
Given for you—you would think, after that,
That nobody would ever cry for ale
Without at least a good tale to trade for it.

Hidden behind the wall, a bell is calling.
All very well for the canons. Up at three
To pray? I'm up at three to put new bread in
And chase the last ropy cockerel round the yard.
This soup's more holy water than cabbage,
Said a man only yesterday. There's chicken
In it, too, I told him, straight. Every day
Save Friday. Then it's fish seethed in milk.
Mistress? Mistress?—God save you,
No more beds here. Go along
To the Slipper Chapel. Say your prayers, pilgrim.
God found Our Lord a bed. Ale, ale.
Let Him—God save us—find you,
By Our Lady, a clean straw bed without fleas.

wendan (to turn)

The Fakenham bus stops beside the pump.
There is one bus for Fakenham on Saturdays.
There are no rooms left to let in the town.
It is the pilgrimage. You understand
And so will flee for Norwich and the train.
London will receive you into its
Surprisingly quiet bosom, after all this:
Tall house in the Crescent, German friends
Laying the long table with broetchen and cheese,
Rooms filled with the brown smell of coffee
And secular calm. There nobody argues over
Comparative qualities of incense, or whether
In an icon Our Lady may appear with the Apostle John—
Her immediate family ONLY, says a man,
Thumping the tea-shop table with clenched fist.

There is the one bus for Fakenham on Saturdays.
It stops beside the pump, and so,
There where the village road's cleft—a forked stick,
Dowsing the way back into the world—
You are waiting with your luggage and your child,
All piled at the foot of the pump like offerings
Retched up from the dark corners of tents
And brought to Aaron to be melted down
While Moses loiters on the cloven mountain—
Silly American family, who forget
Which side of the English road is which,
Silly Americans who have not realized
That the four corners of Norfolk contain the world.

There is the one bus for Fakenham on Saturdays.
When we say, *Stops at the pump,* of course we mean it
Metaphorically. What's literal is that this
Is the weekend for the pilgrimage, and already
People are pouring barefoot into the town
Past the pump, past you, and into the rooms
Where no longer is there any room for you,
And the bus, which stops at the pub across from the pump,
The one Saturday bus, has already gone
Roaring across the sandy hills for Fakenham.

wif (woman)
1323

Thirty to my fourteen: my wedded lord.
The church so cold our white breaths colored

The air, small clouds
The shape of words
I scarcely remembered afterwards.

I was handed onto the horse,
Which shied beneath me. Its rough rackety pace

Bore me east. The hilly road unrolled
Across a mounded field.
Behind me, the long bell tolled.

I practiced marriage. Learned. Then sickness took
Him. The joiner and the cook

Died, too.
I sat beside him through

One watery day, then a night so clear
I could hear

A cock crow across a distant field.
His hand cooled in mine. His face stilled

Into something so unlike itself that I
Already couldn't see

Gray light behind his eyes, the flush
Wind raised in his cheeks. *Flesh of my flesh,*

He called me. *Bone of my bone.*
Now he's stone.

Each morning at Mass
My shadow falls across
His staring face

Graven into the floor. Once
I went back alone and knelt to kiss
The polished slab that keeps his bones in place.

modor (mother)
1235

In dreams I find my Geoffrey up the sycamore.
At his going all the yellow tree-hands clamor.

I can see you down there,
Mother. You're eating up my pear.

My teeth cringe at the grainy-sweet
Fruit-flesh, and at his shout

As he falls from the swagged sky
With a crack and a thud. *Breathe, Mother. Did I die?*

Today he's written to me, black thick-jointed words
That fly across the page like blackbirds

Crying their one foreign syllable,
Perfectly intelligible

To themselves. Shading my eyes with one hand,
I watch them as they bank against the wind

And send their delegations down to roost,
One choir at a time, in the tallest

Yew tree. Sunsets, I hear them
Yammering as the sky drops its hem

Over the red underskirts of day
And wonder what it is they have to say.

sceadu (shadow)

A lost doorway holds a slanted shadow
That looks on a demolished island, fallow

Still in a rare whitewash of moonlight.
Could it live there, with no sun to cast it

But memory, through the quiet rains
These dank spring mornings, across the ordered ruins

Of an older, more disintegrated world
Sinking daily into the wet unplanted field?

Shall the shades rise now and praise?
Does the soul, when it leaves the body's house

And turns the blind corner, sing as it goes?
Does it whistle? Who will listen for the shadows

In their valleys, in their alleyways, at their doors,
As they lean from their mystery into ours?

brimfugol (seabird)
1101

In the morning I hear them crying
As if they had lost their way.
I have never seen the sea.
This morning my lady mistress is dying

And taking her time about it. I have come
From the dim house into the springing green
Of the well garden, to skim
Green scum and frogspawn from the otherwise clean

Well-water—not the holy well.
Yesterday Father Gervais anointed her.
She could not swallow. I think the very ill
Know that soon they will be offered more

Bread and wine, that Christ Himself will feed
Them from His own torn breast.
Christ the bird will tear Himself and bleed,
And truly they at last will feast.

The housefolk don't like it when I loiter
Too long here with the sky-high voices
Crying, *L'eau, l'eau,* above the homely *waeter*,
While the good earth—green and heedless—rejoices.

richeldis
circa 1080

My soul's great with remembering. In my room
I kneel to pray beside the woven pilgrim

Whose flat road stops just short of the raveled
Hem. How odd the untraveled

Air of this world, my own,
Must look to him, all staff and shell and frown.

Stitches fall like footprints across snow
In murky rushlight. Now—

The little flame shivers in the wind.
The curtain's sudden flutter might be a hand

Waving smoke away. Some wing
Treads the dark air, whispering.

My needle's poised, a dragonfly. The window
Stands open to the night. An unfurled shadow

—Owl?— drifts across the moonlit grass.
It seems to me the hand of God could pass

Over this house again and spill
What it will. Its weightless seed swell.

hus (house)

High heaven harrowed a dew-fallow field,
Planted what pleased it. The first building blundered:
Square, Saxon-style. Wrong.
Bad in its bones, the treasure-ship sank.
Each day the doing mocked and unmade me.

Dawn-draft on the dry grass.
The world washed, gray, bending
To summon a singing, a song-rush descending
Of something like wings. A wind-rowing soul
Escaping or coming. A sky-going angel
Sailing the cloud-sea from high heaven's hall,
Door open, then shut again. And is that all?
Through day-dusk, a dim shape
In mist: memory, hope.
But where is she who would keep the house here?
Rope moans on the well-lip. The tree stands bare.

My umaking made this.

Sally Thomas's poetry, fiction, and essays have appeared in *The New Yorker*, *The New Republic*, *First Things*, *Sonora Review*, *Southern Poetry Review*, *Dappled Things*, *The Lost Country*, *Windhover*, and numerous other journals. Her fiction has been shortlisted for the Tuscany Prize for Catholic Fiction and the J.F. Powers Prize for Short Fiction. She is the author of two previous collections of poetry: *Brief Light: Sonnets and Other Small Poems* (Lancelot Books, 2012), and *Fallen Water* (Finishing Line Press, 2015). After sojourns in Utah and Great Britain (the setting for the poems in this collection), she makes her home in the Western Piedmont of North Carolina.

CPSIA information can be obtained
at www.ICGtesting.com
Printed in the USA
LVOW07s0204051116
511756LV00001BA/18/P

9 781635 340259